Hooking Up
with
ADMISSIONS OFFICERS:

Selling Yourself Through College Application Essays

Nancy Frieder

Writing Coach/Editor,

writingcoachhelp.com

Copyright © by 2024 Nancy Frieder

All rights reserved. This book or any of its portion may not be reproduced or transmitted in any means, electronic or mechanical, including recording, photocopying, or by any information storage and retrieval system, without the prior written permission of the copyright holder except in the case of brief quotations embodied in critical reviews and other noncommercial uses permitted by copyright law.

Printed in the United States of America
Library of Congress Control Number: 2024924496
ISBN: Softcover   979-8-89518-518-6
        e-Book   979-8-89518-519-3
Published by: WP Lighthouse
Publication Date: 11/14/2024

To buy a copy of this book, please contact:
WP Lighthouse
Phone: +1-888-668-2459
support@wplighthouse.com
wplighthouse.com

Go get 'em!

Nancy Frieder

WHAT OTHERS ARE SAYING

"Your book/booklet is very well done and your recommendations are practical, clear and right on target.... I don't disagree with any of them, which is a rarity."

-Barry Wanger, President of Wanger Associates, Boston; formerly director of public affairs for Brandeis University; University of California, Santa Barbara; and National Endowment for the Humanities

"I thought (this book) was terrific, and I kept wondering if it had been written by a former admissions officer.... You certainly seem to understand admissions and admissions officers. Great job. The insights you provide should prove helpful to anyone using your book.... I thought your comments were spot-on."

-Paul T. White, JD, Assistant Dean for Admissions, Johns Hopkins University School of Medicine, Baltimore

"I highly recommend this book as a guide for both consultants and students. It is filled with examples that can help consultants guide students through the essay process and assist students both writing and editing their essays."

Cindy Laubenstein, Aspire College and Career Consulting, Atlanta

"We could hear (our son's) voice in his essay. It wasn't like that before he came to you."

-Melissa P., mother

"I loved the conversational, non-intimidating tone. You included almost all of the advice I've heard into one place while still keeping it concise. ... Overall, I think the book is an excellent, comprehensive yet navigable guide to the (college application) process. The tone is a perfect balance between friendly, personal advice and an organized, informative guidebook. It will serve its purpose for students, families and consultants alike."

-Erin Gross, student, Cornell University, Ithaca, NY; and advisor with Students4Students, a college admissions company

"The college admissions officer is looking for an essay that is a true reflection of the applicant. Ms. Frieder's book can teach you how to write an essay that is a true reflection of you!"

-Kathy Urbach, JD, SPHR

Former Assistant Dean, University of Louisville Brandeis School of Law; and University of Florida Levin College of Law.

Remember, you're the bait.

Now go catch an admissions officer.

"The essay portion of the college application was the most frustrating part of the admissions process for both my son and me. Nancy took this over (for me) so that I could shift my son's attention to other critical application deadlines-and it was a wonderful thing."

-Jon S., father and repeat client

Remember, you're the bait. Now go catch an admissions officer.

DEDICATION

First, I dedicate this book to Amy and Josh, who trusted me, and challenged me to remain impartial throughout my guidance. You're the best any mother could hope for. I love you!

Secondly, I dedicate this book to the others who have entrusted me with their personal stories. Although I won't name you, I want to let you know that you have helped me, too. Sometimes your essays, as your English teachers told you, were "good to go," Your bringing me these essays challenged me to find ways to improve them without altering them just for the sake of change. Thus, you've helped me hone my skills. Thank you.

CONTENTS

Part 1
Who are You? 1

1 What do they want? 3

2 The application essay: 8

3 What if I'm just ordinary? 10

4 what's your story? 14

Part 2
The Tools 17

5 Some nuts and bolts of writing 18

6 Top five categories of
grammatical mistakes 26

7 Top five categories of style mistakes 37

8 The top five categories of content problems 43

Part 3
The Finishing Touches 49

9 Working backwards 50

10 The Olympic task of a compelling essay opener 53

11 Getting help 55

12 Word count 58

13 How do I know when I'm finished? 60

ACKNOWLEDGMENTS 63

NOTE TO THE READER

The primary takeaway from Hooking Up With Admissions Officers is to go deep-thinking of yourself as bait to catch the attention of those determining the fate of your application. Each applicant has the power to create refreshing essays by fleshing them out with their own individuality. In other words, don't wait for college to "find yourself." Start looking now.

The central portion of the book is loaded with grammar and style tips. On your first reading of this book, feel free to skim through this section or skip it entirely-- but keep it at hand as you're writing and rewriting. It will be helpful.

In the first and third parts of the book, I alternate my observations about essay writing with my blog posts for Montgomery Community Media, a local news and information outlet. I've included these posts to show readers how I think, rather than to tell them what to think. The blog posts reflect my voice, just as I hope your essays will reflect yours. In addition, I have shared stories about my clients' essays to illustrate specific topics. To protect these students' anonymity and hard work, I've withheld their names and all but excerpts of their writing.

For the sake of simplicity, I discuss the writing prompts only on the College Board's Common Application. Although more than 500 universities currently use the Common Application, many do not. However, the writing prompts usually are broad enough to allow you to tweak your work so you won't have to start from scratch each time you must produce a new essay. The strategies I give for tackling the prompts on the Common App work well for most other application writing prompts, too.

Exceptions are what I call the "CC prompts," the crazy-and-creative-writing ones, required by a few schools, such as the University of Chicago. I'm sure these prompts were designed to throw students for a loop, to see how their minds work--and to determine how much they really want to enroll. If you're applying to a school with CC prompts, you might have to stretch your imagination, but you still can show the admissions officers who you are, what you value or why the school is right for you.

No one can be certain whether his or her essay was the determining factor for an acceptance, but admissions officers say it can be. When applicants have similar test scores and GPAs, the essays are critical-helping them if they're good, hurting them if they're not. If your essays fall in the vast middle ground, you might be at mercy to your luck.

My background is in journalism, not in education. When I help students with their essays, I work as an editor would with a reporter. When I can, I sit beside them, as my first editors did with me, guiding them as they improve their work. The experience is similar online.

Whether I'm helping students locally or from afar, they tell me it "feels different than working with a teacher." Perhaps it's because I help them target their readership and challenge their abilities to delve inside themselves to make the content more meaningful. I also make sure their limited words pack punch.

Students at your level have tight schedules and imminent deadlines. Furthermore, I appreciate everyone's willingness, as I hope my clients appreciate mine, to spend not merely the time required to get the job done, but to spend as much time as needed so we are mutually pleased. Until then, the essay isn't ready. It's a respectful arrangement.

Hooking Up with Admissions Officers should be helpful, but it's not all you will need. I highly recommend having access to a more complete grammar reference, and also having a copy of Strunk and White's The Elements of Style.

The essay may be the most daunting part of the application. I wrote Hooking Up with Admissions Officers to share my experience and insights. The rest is up to you. Go get 'em.

Part 1
Who are You?

1 What do they want?

This is the million dollar question. Why? The best writers target their audience. Thus, you must know what admissions officers want. The good news: They want to know who you are and what you value. The bad news: It's not that simple.

I've found through working locally (in Washington, D.C. area) with seniors from some of the best high schools in the nation, and through working online with teens from other regions, students - especially boys-struggle when writing about themselves. They're far more comfortable with other topics.

You may have excelled at writing academic essays, but application essays are different. If you approach them from an academic standpoint, you might not make the best impression. "But wait!" you might say. "What if I'm applying to an Ivy League school. Don't I need to approach the essay academically?" My answer is emphatically no.

Don't get me wrong; I'm not implying you shouldn't care about grammar and writing skills. Quality counts! What I'm strongly suggesting is that a college application essay is far different from an academic one.

I've seen many essays that AP English teachers had given A's to that likely wouldn't have caught an admissions officer's attention without changes. To make a memorable first impression, you must understand the differences between academic and application essays. This chart should help:

Academic vs. Application Essays

	Academic Essay	Application Essay
Personal Tone	Stick to formal writing	Sound like your speaking Tone voice, but don't speak like an idiot (How would you speak to your aunt?)
External Sources	Expected	Usually optional. Your Perspective is paramount.
Opening Paragraph	Strong thesis Statement introducing what the Essay will cover	A hook for the reader's attention or curiosity. Think "story opening rather than "school assignment".
Body	Thoughts should be Organized in paragraphs. Each paragraph should move the piece forward	Same

| Closing Paragraph | Wrap up the essay, rewording and reinforcing your opening paragraph. | Think of how you end a story or joke. The best endings tie into the opening paragraph, leaving the reader satisfied or "wowed!" |

From coast to coast, whether you're applying to an Ivy League school or to a state university, admissions officers want to know who you really are. This is important. The test scores and GPAs tell only so much. Moreover, with thousands of students with the same or similar numbers applying to each school, the essay provides one of the best means for discovering who "fits." If their numbers are within the school's range, students who best can tell admissions officers who they are within the given word-count restrictions have the greatest shot at being accepted.

The essay matters more than ever. Despite what some may think, admissions officers are human. Humans have emotions and are wired for good stories. Take advantage of this when writing the essay. However, be careful not to give the admissions officers a sob story (parental divorce, death, not making the team, etc.), especially if it's one that many others might share.

Many college counselors and advisors tell students to avoid such topics at all costs. I disagree. The topic isn't the problem; it's how the writer approaches it. In my opinion, writing about being a child of divorce is like walking through a minefield. Take care not to step on the trap of turning the essay into a sob story about how you overcame a heart-rendering situation. Instead, show the reader how it built your character.

A few years ago, I was assisting a young man who wanted to write about how his parents' divorce, when he was seven, affected him currently. The essay began from the eyes of a seven-year-old but quickly moved forward.

The boy lived with his mother, but he looked forward to Occasional lunch outings with his dad. Sometimes, however, his father's credit cards wouldn't work. Thus, the boy would have to call his mom to pay for their meals. "How horrible," I thought. I felt bad for both the boy and his mother for having ties to such a deadbeat.

But the beauty of the essay was the student didn't relay it as sob story. Instead, he demonstrated how he had learned, as he

got older, to bring money he had earned "just in case." He lovingly didn't want to embarrass his dad by having to call his mom to bail them out. Thus, he learned the importance of always being prepared, and he relayed it to other elements of his life. In effect, this student turned a story that easily could have been pathetic into a powerfully empathetic depiction of growth, maturity and problem solving.

Another example of dodging a dangerously overdone topic was my experience in helping a student who wanted to write his essay about not qualifying for a basketball team. His first draft would have had admissions officers rolling their eyes and whimpering to themselves, "Oh no. Not another one!" But a tiny detail caught my eye, and I saw it as an means to transform the essay into something more palatable and enlightening.

In the student's first version, he briefly had mentioned that when his name was finally called, his relief was quickly shattered upon learning he had been selected merely for the practice team.

His humiliation escalated when he learned, as a practice player, he wouldn't receive a team jersey.

I recommended he rewrite his essay to highlight this different angle. His new opening paragraph went something like this:

> Some people say clothes make the man.
> In my case, it was a shirt.

Then he relayed the story of his determination, which eventually earned him a jersey and a place on the team. It was an effective piece, which if told more traditionally, would have been just another "finally-making-the-team" essay.

In a nutshell, admissions officers want to feel as though they've had a chance to meet the applicant. To achieve this, you must be introspective. Without a thorough self-examination, you're just one of many thousands of applicants. With it, you become a unique individual who happens to be applying to the school.

2. The application essay:

A dream or nightmare?

http://www.mymcmedia.org/college-application-essay-a-dream-or-nightmare/

Blog Post: Aug. 30, 2013

The 50-year anniversary of the March on Washington led by the Rev. Dr. Martin Luther King Jr. has gathered attention in the news. Now this may seem a little strange, but it reminds me of college application says. Perhaps you're thinking that I'm taking this too far, Or that I need to take a break  from being a writing coach. But bearme here, and I'll explain.

Like Dr. King's speech from the steps of the Lincoln Memorial, many essays I've seen are filled with students' dreams: dreams of their future and dreams of their role in making the world a better place. And these dream-filled essays.

come from even the most analytical people, such as those applying to engineering programs at schools at Michigan or MIT.

Is this a good thing? You bet. There's a place for planning and a place for dreaming. The application essay is a place in which the student not only can-but should allow his or her dreams to soar.

How inspirational would Dr. King's speech have been if he had said, "I have a plan..."? Not very, I suppose.

When Dr. King spoke of his dream, it was inspirational not just to the people who shared his dream, but to all people with dreams of their own and dreams for their children. Likewise, when college applicants write about their dreams, admissions officers can relate because they also were once at this fork-in-the-road of life between high school and college, student and professional, youth and adulthood. Dreams may differ, but we all have them; they're what make us human.

Admissions officers see many applicants with similar GPAs and test scores. The applicant who can write an essay that reflects his or her individuality through an interesting story will capture attention. Believe it or not, admissions officers are human, and some of their decisions, when you get right down to it, are emotional. If they like you, they'll want you at their school. Don't get me wrong; I'm not saying the numbers aren't important. I'm saying admissions officers often turn to the GPA and test scores to rationalize their emotional decisions. Do you see the importance of the essay in the application process, especially when the GPAs and test scores are similar among applicants? I can't emphasize this enough: The essay can make the difference between acceptance and rejection. Think about it.

So plan on how you will finance your education and your educational path, but let your dreams radiate in your essay. However, you'll have to be more subtle than declaring "I have a dream...." That line already has been most notably taken.

3 What if I'm just ordinary?

I hear this a lot. Even parents ask me, "What should an ordinary student write about?" I think they're stressing out rather than looking for answers. In fact, some of these very parents are the first to brag about their sons and daughters at other times. I know many so-called ordinary students who've enrolled in Ivy League or other competitive schools. The difference between ordinary and extraordinary often is putting in a little "extra."

For the most part, application writing prompts are designed for one purpose: to discover who the applicants are. This includes how they think, what they value and how they react to various situations. In other words, delve deeply within yourself to produce the type of essay the admissions officers seek.

It seems to me that nobody and everybody are ordinary. top worrying about that. But parents will be parents; you can't change that. So let's forget about them for now. Instead, concentrate on learning more about yourself. It's not just good the application, it's good for you. You might even want to have your essays to look back upon in 10 or 20 years to see how you've grown.

In general, application writing prompts are intended to prod you into exploring you inner self, which gives schools information they can't gather from test scores, GPAs or extracurricular activities. Therefore, you must address each prompt's purpose with care. The following is an overview of the current prompts on the College Board's Common Application, used for applying to more than 500 schools. My comments follow each prompt.

Writing Prompts on the Common App

1. Some students have a background or story that is so central to their identity that they believe their application would be incomplete without it. If this sounds like you, then please share your story.

   Make sure your story is distinctively yours. Even if others share a similar story, strive to show how yours or your perspective of it-is unique. Most importantly, analyze this influence on your character.

2. Recount an incident or time when you experienced failure. How did it affect you, and what lessons did you learn?

   Analyze an experience that illustrates your character and how this will relate to you at this school or in your life.

3. Reflect on a time when you challenged a belief or idea. What prompted you to act? Would you make the same decision again?

   This prompt seeks your introspect and retrospect. The word "reflect" implies its desire for an introspective response. Dig deep, especially when determining what prompted you. Apply equal thought into the retrospective portion of your response. Select a good story.

4. Describe a place or environment where you are perfectly content. What do you do or experience there, and why is it meaningful to you?

> Get personal and specific about the setting. Try showing how you feel rather than simply telling it Determine the significance of your feelings. Admissions officers want you to soul-search.

5. Discuss an accomplishment or event, formal or informal, that marked your transition from childhood to adulthood within you culture, community or family.

> Specifically describe the transition, being analytical about yourself. How do you fit into or distinguish yourself within a larger social unit?

Each year on Aug. 1, the Common Application goes online. Once school starts, finding time for the essays becomes more difficult. Sacrificing a day or two or even few hours of your summer will pay off in the fall. If you're aiming for selective schools, rushing through your essays could be disastrous. Thinking, writing and rewriting take time.

Find someone else to look at your work. Many top students writing consultants. At the very least, show the essay to a reader, family member or trusted friend.

Don't trust this job to those who will report liking it no what and Not should you select someone who enjoys finding good. Knowing what to leave in is as important as knowing what of change. Ideally, find someone knowledgeable enough to offer you a solid, honest critique.

Remember, the essay is yours. Listen to other's suggestions, but don't follow them blindly. The essay is the reflection you will give to the admissions office. Be pleased with it.

4 what's your story?

http://www.mymcmedia.org/whats-your-story-2/

Blog Post: Aug. 25, 2014

Today is the first day of school. Yesterday's rising seniors are now in their final year of high school. This will be a year to k back on with fond memories. But living it is another story. Speaking of stories, how's that college application essay coming along?

Before football season ends, the early application deadline will have passed. And like it or not, the early deadline is getting to be the norm. Colleges report an increasing number of students are plying early, especially non-binding early action. Why? It a better chance of acceptance. Here in Maryland, the College Park campus requires students to apply early to be considered for its honors and scholars programs.

Most of the applications are fairly straightforward. The book, however, require much thought and introspection. Application essays are not like academic essays, in which one.

Researches, jots down some facts, organizes and writes. If you want the admissions officers to notice your application among the hundreds-if not thousands-they review, you'd better have an impressive essay.

Take control. Think of your essay as an opportunity to tell your own story. That's what the admissions officers want. They know your test scores and GPA, but they don't know what kind of person you are. How do you think? How do you react in certain situations? What do you value? The College Board designed its writing prompts to generate these kinds of responses.

Don't fall flat by not delving into your soul to produce the kind of essays admissions officers seek. The best ones I've seen and I've seen a lot-were sweated out over time rather than cranked out. But even the ones that were written quickly required rewrites and edits. So don't procrastinate.

Remember, it's your story. I have worked with a variety of students over the past few years. I always clarify that the student is the writer; I'm just the coach. They can take or leave my suggestions because the essays are theirs. They own them. Sure, they're showing them to the colleges, but they belong to the applicants.

The essays, while certainly challenging, become less of a chore when you think of them as time capsules that, in 10 or 20 years, will tell you how much you have changed or stayed the same. If you approach your essays this way, you will produce more honest, introspective work-precisely what the admissions officers want.

It's equally important to know what the admissions officers don't want: the three B's of boredom, bragging and bad writing. Bragging and bad writing are fairly self-explanatory, so I'll just focus on avoiding boredom for now.

The best way to keep from boring the admissions officer is to make sure your story is a good one. Don't think essay; think story.

What makes a good story? It's not just something that engages the audience. It's something with a big hook at the beginning, some kind of conflict or challenge, and a resolution that makes the whole thing memorable. Some people compare telling a good story with telling a good joke. From the very beginning, you must know where it's leading, or else you'll kill the punchline. The same holds true with writing the college application essay. It must have purpose.

So if you haven't started yet, go find the writing prompt that beckons you. Delve into your soul. And remember: Don't procrastinate. Good essay writers don't scrimp on their sweat or time.

Part 2
The Tools

5 Some nuts and bolts of writing

Warning: You're beginning the heaviest portion of this book. Trust me, learning this will pay off.

If youhad been required to learn the foundations of grammar same way you had to learn your multiplication tables, you ild have progressed to higher writing levels in the same way moved on to long division, algebra and perhaps calculus.

Here's a review:

The Parts of Speech:

Noun	The name of a person Place, thing, idea or Quality	Jenna lives in Chicago, Movies provide entertainment People enjoy vacations
Pronoun	Takes the place of a noun	Jake lost his phone. The snake shed its skin. Sue saw her coaches and told them she would miss practice.

Verb	Expresses action, being or state of being	Jeff left the room. Julia is a doctor. Bigotry still exists.
Adjective	describes a noun or pronoun Or another adverb (it may be A word, phrase or clause)	I have a cute dog. The man in the shower was singing (adj. phrase)
Adverb	describes a verb, adjective Or another adverb (it may Be a word, phrase or clause)	She spoke softly. The boy walked into the room. (adj phse)
Preposition	Shows a relation between its object and some other word in the sentence.	They hiked through the rainforest. (Through shows the nature between rainforest. It's object, and hiked, the verb.
Conjunction	connects words or groups of groups	Amy and Josh are at school. I ran but couldn't catch him.
Interjection	expresses strong feeling	Ouch! Darn! Oh!

What You Should Know About Nouns and Pronouns

Nouns and pronouns have gender, person, number and ease. Gender is easy. Nouns and pronouns can be masculine (he), feminine (her), neither (a desk) or either (a student).

Person generally comes naturally in speech and determines which pronoun will be used. First person denotes the person speaking. (1, John King, accept the challenge.) Second person denotes the person or thing spoken to. (You, young man, should be ashamed.) Third person denotes the person or thing spoken of. Nouns used alone are always in the third person. (Our teacher is here. She will help us.) Students commonly learn about person through literature, by determining whether a book is narrated in first or third-person.

Number is singular or plural. As straight forward as it sems, be careful. Some nouns take the same form whether singular or plural (sheep, deer, trout, etc.). Subject and verbs

t be consistent in number. Some nouns are plural in form but singular in use (measles, news, summons, etc.).

Take note that media is the plural of medium. Anyone who knows grammar will not say the media is biased. However, they correctly might say the media are biased.

With few exceptions, people rarely struggle with gender,of number. Case, however, is a problem. The schools, in opinion, don't teach the concept well. This leads to many grammatical problems I encounter in the essays.

The case of a noun or pronoun shows its relationship to other in the sentence. Nouns and pronouns have three cases: native, objective and possessive. I believe teachers adequate lessons on the possessive case, so I won't drag details. However, I feel the other two cases frequently are Except for possessive nouns, nouns don't change dam with case changes, but pronouns do. If you grasp this concept, you'll avoid many of mistakes I find in application essays

I have a dear friend who always employs the wrong case when using pronouns after prepositions. For instance, if I ask her whether she has our tickets for an upcoming ballgame, she may respond: "Not yet, but Mark will give them to Brian and I when we see him tomorrow night." I cringe but don't correct her. I'm much more lenient regarding conversational English than I am with the written word.

My friend had learned to say "so-and-so and I" in school rather than "so-and-so and me." However, this is correct only in the nominative case. So let's examine the basics so we can move on. First, let's look at the most common pronouns in each of their case forms:

Personal Pronouns

Nominative	Objective	Possesive
I	Me	my, mine
You (sing)	You (sing)	your (sing)
He, she or it	him, her or it	his, her
We	us	our, ours
You	you	your, yours
They	them	their, theirs

Pronouns may seem simple to the native speaker, but they can become complicated. There are many kinds of pronouns other than personal pronouns. For instance, relative (or conjunctive) pronouns, serve also as connecting words. Relative pronouns can serve as a subject, or as the object of a verb or preposition.

It's important to apply these pronouns correctly not only for the college admissions offices, but for any writing in which one wants to be taken seriously. If readers recognize the writing as being sloppy, couldn't they subconsciously infer that lack of care would transfer to the thought behind it?

Who or Whom?

(relative pronouns, both singular and plural)

Nominative	Objective	Possessive
Who	Whom	Whose

People who understand how to use the various cases will know when to use who or whom (or whoever or whomever).

When to Use Each Case

Nominative	when it's the subject of the sentence	Who won the game? We won the game
	when it follows some form of "to be" (is, was, were, been)	She was thought to be grammatically correct, but awkward. ("She was mistaken for me" sounds better. Notice it's in the objective case now because it's the object of the preposition "for")

Objective	when it's the object of a Preposition	She was the One for whom I was looking.
	When it's the direct object (receive of he verb)	He rubbed *her* the wrong way.
	When it's indirect object usually follows the direct objects but, if not, it can be changed to a prepositional phrase using "to" or "for.	He bought dinner her. He bought her dinner.
Possessive	shows ownership	He borrowed my book.
	Introducing a gerund (an action verb that act Like a noun)	His snoring annoyed me.

What You Should Know About Verbs

The two most crucial parts of a sentence are its subject (usually a noun or pronoun) and its verb. Everything else is window dressing. Verbs usually create the interest in the sentence. Select them wisely.

Description is great, but admissions officers will get bored with essays padded with adjectives and adverbs. Moreover, too many colorful words will eat up the limited word count, preventing more important information. If possible, choose verbs that provide description without needing an adjective. For instance, "The convict fled" is a stronger sentence than "The convict ran quickly away," and it shaves off two words. That's significant. Given the same subject matter, admissions officers prefer tightly written essays over pieces that take up more of their time.

Most students recognize verbs, including linking or auxiliary verbs. Furthermore, most people are comfortable with irregular verbs, which stray from the regular verb forms by not simply adding a d or ed to form their past tense or past participle. However, some irregular verbs-notoriously lay and lie- continue to wreak havoc for most people.

First, I want to discuss what teachers seldom tell their students: Verbs not only can be classified as regular or irregular, they can be transitive, intransitive or sometimes both. Transitive verbs require a direct object (a receiver of the action); intransitive verbs do not.

Transitive	Intransitive	Both
I made my bed.	Water evaporates.	We threw (tr.) the ball
Mike has a toothache.	Jessica runs quickly.	He threw (intr.) up.

When the subject performs the action, the sentence is in the active voice. When the subject receives action, the sentence is in the passive voice.

Strive to write in the active voice because it better serves the reader. The result tends to be tighter, and the sentences are more clear, engaging and powerful.

When a sentence or clause ends in "by" somebody, or if it could end that way, the sentence is likely to be in the passive voice. In the following examples, the first sentence is active. The subject performs the action. The other examples are passive:

> Adam caught the ball.
> The ball was caught by Adam.
> The ball was caught.

The second sentence gives as much information as the first, but it has two more words. In addition, the construction is awkward. The sentence tends to interest the reader more when the subject (Adam) performs the action.

The third sentence is the worst. The subject again is the ball, and we know it was caught. But that's all we know. Who caught it? This structure should be avoided unless there's a reason for obscuring who performed the action. For instance, when political mishaps occur, press agents commonly release a statement that "mistakes were made."

Speaking of mistakes, I'd like to address the most frequent blunders in grammar, style and content I encounter when helping students with their essays.

6 Top five categories of grammatical mistakes

1.) Problem Words

English has many misused words. Here are some of them:

To lay or to lie?

The verb to lie (to tell a falsehood) is a regular verb. But the irregular verbs to lay or to lie mean something else, and they are entirely different from each other. If they confuse you, you never learned the grammar behind them. Don't simply remember that you "lie down in bed" and "lay a book on the table." If you do, your focus will be on the bed, book or table whenever you come across lay or lie.

Forget that lesson. It's too confusing and often doesn't work. Think about lay as being a transitive verb, meaning that it needs an object to complete the sentence. To lie is always intransitive. Now you can understand why one "lays a book (the direct object) on the table" but "lies in bed." Furthermore, you won't get confused about "laying your weary body direct object) in bed" next to a "book lying on the table."

While to lie is always an intransitive verb, to lay is usually transitive except when used in context with hens. It's correct to say a hen lays well. (If your mind is wandering, I won't go there!)

The present tense is fairly simple when you consider these two verbs in terms of being transitive or intransitive. However, both are irregular verbs, and the nature of their past tense and past participle forms may be confusing.

Sometimes, especially with tricky words, it's best to tackle the grammar as you would in learning a foreign language. Confusion about many tricky words subsides upon understanding conjugation, case, and the different kinds of verbs.

To Lay

	Present tense	Past tense	Past/present/ participate
I	lay	laid	laid/laying
You (sing)	lay	laid	laid/laying
He, she or it	lays	laid	laid/laying
We	lay	laid	laid/laying
You (pi.)	lay	laid	laid/laying
They	lay	laid	laid/laying

To Lie
(intransitive verb meaning to recline)

	Present tense	Past tense	Past/present/ participate
I	lie	laid	lain / lying
You	lie	laid	lain / lying
He, she or it	lies	laid	lain / lying
We	lie	laid	lain / lying
You (pi.)	lie	laid	lain / lying
They	lie	laid	lain / lying

Knowing a word's past participle is crucial for forming the present perfect (He has laid it down), past perfect (He had laid it down) and future perfect tenses (He will have laid it down).

Who or whom?

Although I covered this on pages 22-23 (refer to it, if necessary), I'd like to add a few remarks. If you ever get confused on which form to use, try substituting another pronoun in its nominative or objective case. For instance, if substituting she (a nominative pronoun) works in the sentence, the correct form should be who (also a nominative pronoun). Likewise, if her (an objective pronoun) works, the correct form should be whom.

Be careful when the sentence with who or whom has two or more clauses. (A clause is a group of words that has both a subject and a predicate. Remember, the predicate is the portion of the sentence that includes the verb.) The determining factor of whether the relative pronoun should be who or whom depends upon its use within the clause. For example:

She is the person who/whom found my cat.

[She is the person] [who found my cat]. (Select the nominative case because its role is the subject of the clause.)

The woman who/whom you saw is my mother. The woman [whom you saw] is my mother. (Select the objective case because its role is the object of saw.)

Don't forget, always use the nominative case when the word in question follows a linking verb. Just as you would say this is she, you also would say this is who.

Also, be sure to use some form of who or whom when referring to a person. Saying "the person that" rather than "the person who" is an easy mistake to fall into.

Which or that?

When the portion of the sentence is not essential, merely descriptive, use which, and precede it with a comma. When the portion is essential to the sentence, use that. Do not precede it a comma.

If I were to give you directions to my house, I might conclude by saying, "It's the fifth house on the right, which has brown shutters." Upon turning on to my street, you would count the five houses on the right. The fifth house would have brown shutters, but that information isn't necessary.

If I were to say, "It's the fifth house of the right that has brown shutters," the person would need to count only the houses on the right with brown shutters. My house could be the twentieth.

It's or Its?

It's is the contraction for it is. (It's cold outside.) Its is a possessive pronoun. (The cat groomed its fur.)

There, They're or Their?

This reminds me of a joke: How to you comfort editors? Pat them on the back, and say "there, they're, their!"

There can serve as an introductory word, technically known As an expletive. (There are more girls than boys in the class.) There also can be an adverb, showing place. (My keys are over there.)

They're is the contraction for they are. (They're Mets fans.)

Their is a pronoun. (Their mother is a lawyer.)

Less or Fewer?

Less indicates amount, rather than something one can count. (We hoped for less snow this year.)

Fewer indicates number. It's countable. (Schools in Tennessee have fewer snow days than schools in Michigan.)

Affect or Effect?

Affect is almost always a verb, meaning to influence. (My SAT scores will affect which schools I will apply to.) In rare Cases associated with psychology, affect can be a noun. Be aware of that, but you'll not likely use it in that sense.

Effect can be a noun or verb.

As a noun, it means a result. (One of the effects of 9/11 was increased airport security.)

As a verb, it means to bring about. (Increases in alumni donations effect increases in scholarships and renovations.)

Compare to, or Compare with?

Comparing to points out similarities between things that are generally considered different. (The disgruntled citizen Compared the United States to ancient Rome.)

Compared with points out differences between things that are generally considered similar. (When we went car shopping, we compared Toyotas with Hondas.)

2.) Shifts in Structure

Shifts in structure cause awkward sentences. Avoid these:

Shifts in person:
One must study if one (not you) wants to get good grades.

Shifts in number:
One should do one's (not their) best.

Shifts in voice:
As we drove down the road, we saw a lemonade stand (not a lemonade stand was seen).

Shifts in tense:
My mother came home from work and made (not makes) dinner.

Shifts in subject:
Julia's sweaters are eye-catching because they are colorful (not because she has good taste).

3.) Pronoun Case

This is a widespread problem. (Review pages 20-23.)

4.) Dangling and Misplaced Modifiers

A modifier (whether a participle phrase or a prepositional phase) must be next to the word it's modifying. If it's in a phrase at the beginning of a sentence in which the subject of the sentence doesn't directly follow it, the modifier is said to be dangling. If it's not at the beginning but separated from the word it's modifying, it's misplaced.

Remember, a preposition shows a relationship, such as over, under, inside, outside, through, upon, etc.

A participle is a form of a verb that has some of the properties of a verb (it can take an object) and some of the properties of an adjective (it can modify a noun or pronoun).

Present participles end in ing and generally describe an action occurring at the same time as another action. (Standing by the window, I watch cars go by.) Sometimes present participles can refer to a time past. (Standing by the window, I

Aw cars go by.)

Past participles generally indicate a completed action. The past participle of a regular verb usually has the same form as the past tense. (He knocks on the door. He knocked on the door. He had knocked on the door.) However, irregular verbs have past participles with various changes in form. (I see the car. I saw the car. I have seen the car.)

Sometimes dangling and misplaced modifiers can be funny. At the very least, they can confuse the reader.

The classic comedian Groucho Marx had a line that took advantage of a misplaced modifier:

I shot an elephant in my pajamas. How he got into my pajamas, I'll never know.

The sentence is comically unclear because the prepositional phrase (in my pajamas) appears to modify the direct object (the elephant) rather than the subject of the sentence (I). Rewording it to "In my pajamas, I shot an elephant" fixes the problem.

Make sure the modifier is next to the word it's modifying.

Not all misplaced modifiers are as funny as Groucho Marx's, but I catch them frequently.

The dangling participle is another kind of a misplaced modifier:

Hanging from a tree, I picked the most beautiful apple.

That sentence is unclear because it seems like the subject, who directly follows the participle phrase, is hanging from the tree. Rewording the sentence to "I picked the most beautiful apple hanging from the tree" fixes the problem.

Be careful whenever starting a sentence with a present participle. Dangling participles are extremely common.

5.) Subject-Verb Agreement:

If the subject is singular (or plural), the verb must be in the matching form. However, certain sentence formations cause confusion. Here are the rules:

Words joined to a subject by with, accompanied by, together with, as well as, no less than or including do not change the number of the subject:

The teacher, as well as the students, watched the video.
The students, as well as the teacher, watched the video.

Two or more singular subjects joined by or or nor take a singular verb:

Either Jake or Susan is the winner of the contest. Neither Michael nor Jonathan plays on the team.

When a subject comprises both singular and plural forms joined by or or nor, the verb must agree with the form closer to the subject:

> Either Jake or we are the winners of the contest.
> Either we or Jake is the winner of the contest.
> Neither the coach nor the players want to practice today.
> Neither the players nor the coach wants to practice today.

In a sentence beginning with here or there, the number of the verb depends on what follows it:

> There is a book on the desk
> There are books on the desk.
> Here is my brother.
> There go my parents.

Collective nouns, which are singular in form but name a group or collection, take singular verbs when they are considered a unit. However, they take plural verbs when the individuals are considered:

> The football team has a winning record.
> The graduating class have received their diplomas.

In expressions such as one of the girls who or one of the books that, the verb in the relative clause agrees with the antecedent of the relative clause. Remember, clauses contain both a subject and a predicate (the part of the sentence that includes the verb). Phrases do nothave both

Relative clauses are introduced by a relative pronoun-who, whom, whose, which and that:

The grilled fish platter is one of the main courses that have fewer than 1,000 calories. (The antecedent of that is main courses.) The grilled fish platter is the only one of the main courses that has fewer than 1,000 calories. (The antecedent of that is the only one.)

However, a phrase between the subject and the verb (except when following a relative clause) does not affect the verb:

One of the cats belongs to my neighbor.

Each, either, neither, someone, somebody, anyone, anybody, everyone, everybody, no one, nobody, none, one and a person are singular.

Each of the suspects was questioned. Neither Bob nor Kayla was at the party.

If plenty, abundance or rest is modified by a phrase introduced with of, the verb agrees with the noun in the phrase:

Plenty of dogs learn tricks.
An abundance of clothing was donated.

Fractions are used in this same way:

Half of the project is finished.
One third of the teachers are men.

If the word number is preceded by a and followed by of, it requires a plural verb; if it is preceded by the, it requires a singular verb:

A number of tourists were from Europe.
The number of European tourists is high.

A noun that refers to an amount of money, a space of time or a unity of measurement is singular in meaning even though the form is plural:

> Ten dollars is the cost of admission.
> Three hours is a long time to wait.
> Twenty-five miles is a full day's hike.

If the subject of the verb is made up of two or more words connected by and, the verb is plural. However, if the two words are considered a unit, the verb is singular:

> Carrot cake and apple pie are his favorite desserts.
> Peanut butter and jelly is his favorite sandwich.

If a subject has two or more nouns but only one is expressed, the verb is plural:

A Canon and Nikon camera are for sale.

7 Top five categories of style mistakes

Mistakes in grammar are undeniable blunders. Style mistakes, however, fall into a grayer area of writing unless you're writing for a publication with specific guidelines. When working on your college application essays, you have more leeway than other writers, yet you still should apply the principles of good style.

Essays with style deficits may not be technically "wrong," but they are more laborious to read. For a college admission officer who must sift through thousands of essays, poor style can make the difference between acceptance and rejection. I strongly recommend avoiding the following style mistakes when possible:

1.) Redundancy

Purposeful redundancy for emphasis is good when used sparingly. (Brandon is bored-bored with his job, bored with his friends and bored with his life.) However, an essay full of redundancies not only can be tiring to read, but it can eat up precious word space for communicating important ideas.

When you choose a strong verb, certain adjectives or adverbs can be redundant. What's the difference between obliterating something and totally obliterating it? Verbs, being words of action, form more interesting sentences than any other part of speech. Using a descriptive verb is better than using an embellished weaker one. Draw on adjectives or adverbs when necessary, but don't let them divert a powerful verb's impact.

Using pronouns is another way to avoid redundancy in writing. Once you've completed your essay or have gotten to a stopping point, read it aloud. Does it sound the way you speak? When you don't apply enough pronouns, your essay sounds repetitious.

On the other hand, if you use too many pronouns, you will confuse the reader. Reading the essay aloud solves this problem,

Sometimes the topic itself becomes redundant. Knowing when to move on or when to end the essay is critical. Sometimes It's just a matter of when it feels right.

Find others to read your work, but choose your readers with care. Ideally they'll be knowledgeable, but make sure they're at least trustworthy. (See Chapter 10 for recommendations.)

2.) Overusing the Passive Voice

Although it's technically not wrong to use the passive voice, exercise caution and extreme moderation. In general, avoid it. When the subject of the sentence performs the action sentence is more natural, easier to read and more clear. Such a sentence is in the active voice.

When the subject of a sentence is the receiver of the action, the sentence usually is wordier and weaker. Sometimes the reader can't determine who or what performed the action. Such a sentence is in the passive voice. (See page 25 for more details.)

3) Not Being Concise

Distracting people is relatively easy. Magicians employ it to perform their tricks. Readers, including college admissions officers, can lose focus or interest if the writer doesn't take certain precautions.

You may submit a well thought-out essay that's grammatically perfect. However, the brutal truth is, if the admissions officer doesn't enjoy it, you may not be accepted to the school.

Admissions officers are busy; they have stacks of essays to get through every day of the admissions season. Be kind to them. Without knowing them personally, you may not know their particular likes, but you know they want to learn about you (see Chapter 1). Do your utmost to ensure your work is easy to read.

I'm not advocating talking down to them. I'm suggesting making every word count. Don't overload them with too many adjectives or adverbs (see page 24). Of course, avoid being redundant and using the passive voice.

An editor's trick of the trade for making a piece more concise is to rid the copy of extraneous thats. For instance:

Jeff told Bill that Sherri said that she could come to the party.
Jeff told Bill Sherri said she could come to the party.
Jeff told Bill Sherri could come to the party.

Nothing about the second sentence changes from the first when the two extraneous thats disappear. Not only do they increase the word count, but they can erode an admissions officer's interest over the course of reading the essay. Don't wear out an admission officer with extra words.

The third sentence shows further editing. However, be careful when taking this step because it could change the waning somewhat. For instance, leave the second sentence alone if it was important for Jeff to report Sherri's telling him. she could come. Otherwise, the third sentence is better.

4.) Lack of Variety

You can use many techniques to spice up your writing. Sentences can be straightforward, or they can begin with various types of clauses or phrases. Read your words aloud and listen for monotonous structure. For instance:

> I went to the store to buy a new outfit. I found a nice pair of jeans and a cool shirt. I will wear my new outfit to Jordan's party.

> Shopping for a new outfit, I found a nice pair of jeans and a cool shirt at the store. I'll wear them to Jordan's party.

Alternative longer sentences in a paragraph with shorter ones also makes the writing more interesting. The previous Example demonstrates that, too.

5.) Not Emphasizing Something Well

One of my favorite quotes on writing comes from Mark Twain:

"Substitute 'damn' every time you're inclined to write 'very;' your editor will delete it and the writing will be just as it should be."

Students often rely on very for emphasis. This redundancy isn't very frustrating for readers, it's exasperating. Do you see how one good word takes the place of two? Don't forget, admissions officers tire and get bored easily. Extra words add up. Whenever you find a more powerful word to take the place of multiple words, you're both writing better and doing the reader and ultimately yourself a favor.

A word's placement has an effect on its emphasis. Placing the word to be stressed at the beginning or end of the sentence can draw attention to it. For instance:

> The soldiers, after a long battle, triumphed when they secured the bridge.
>
> After a long battle, the soldiers secured the bridge and triumphed.

Another way to emphasize is to be climatic. Whenever there is a list (having three items works best), make sure the last is the most impactful.

I helped a student applying to the University of Chicago, which is notorious for its crazy writing prompts. The student was asked to compare apples and oranges. He maintained that although they both are fruits, they should not be compared. I won't go into the details of his essay, but I'll reveal his last paragraph, which demonstrates climatic emphasis:

> The apple and the orange, both enticing and healthy fruits, should most definitely not be compared because of the level of complexity and uniqueness that exists in each. The tremendous difference in flavor should be enough to render them incomparable. Would we compare a Kit Kat to a Twix bar just because they are made of chocolate?

Would we compare an Android to an iOS just because they are renowned operating systems? Should we compare our children?

Another way to show emphasis is through repetition. It can work well, but beware of becoming redundant. (See page 39.)

8 The top five categories of content problems

1.) Fear of Telling a Personal Story

One of the best ways to avoid boring admissions officers is to tell them a personal story. Contrary to what some students may believe, admissions officers are human and, thus, wired for listening to good stories. Entertain them with your insight.

Be personal but not too personal. The application essay is no place to recount stories of your love life. Avoid sob stories (see page 5-6) unless they provide deep insight or unique twists.

I helped a student once who insistently struggled through an essay that made him sound like any one of thousands of good students out there. He looked at me and sighed, "I wish I had the nerve to tell the story about what happened to me at my aunt and uncle's lake house." When he told me the story, I knew he should write about it. His hesitation was due to a painful lesson he had learned. It was a perfect essay. We had an opening paragraph that hooked the reader, and an unforgettable ending. I loved it.

In the end, the student opted to submit his ordinary essay. I advised him against it, but it was his application. Other students overcame their fears, but I'll never forget the one who didn't.

2.) Lame Attempts at Humor

Few things are less funny than someone trying to be humorous but failing. No matter how amusing your friends think you are, don't try to write a funny essay. Think about your audience (the admissions officers) and what they're doing (reading lots of essays).

Professional comedians know the value of a good warm-up act. The audience needs to be primed for laughter. Admissions officers are nowhere near primed. They simply want to get a good idea of who's applying to the school.

The best places to slip in personality or humor are the opening and closing paragraphs. Keep the body of the essay thought provoking and structured. If it sounds like the real you, the essay is on track.

3.) Disorganization

Applications essays, just like academic essays, must be organized. Creating an outline takes a few minutes upfront, but doing so saves time overall. Outlines are rudimentary road maps, keeping writers from losing course as they flesh out the details.

Many schools teach the "hamburger method" of writing. The introduction is compared to the top section of the bun, and the "meat" consists of roughly three paragraphs that explain the opening paragraph. The last paragraph, the bottom portion of the bun, wraps up the essay by rewording the introduction.

Students who use the hamburger method for their application essays might not write bad essays, but they generally don't write powerful ones either.

Don't think about hamburgers when writing application essays; think about fishing. Make sure your pole has a strong hook and enticing bait. The purpose of the opening paragraph in this type of essay is not necessarily to introduce the body of your work directly. It's to catch fish, the admissions officers.

Once you've baited your hook, don't let any potential fish slip away. Reel them in with your story. Slip-ups in grammar, spelling or style can result in their getting away. This part, the body of your essay, is basically the same as the meat of the academic essay. The main difference lies in the importance of the application essay's pace, which you should set to sound as though you're telling the story yourself. In fact, you are.

When the time comes to reel the fish in, make sure your ending is spectacular. Obviously, admissions officers aren't fish. Your nabbing them won't kill them; on the contrary, they're dying for applicants to catch them. Aim for your story to be the fishing tale the admissions officers will want to relay to others.

4.) Telling More About the Passion or Hero Than About Oneself

This is a huge stumbling block. If you're writing about something or someone you're so passionate about that your writing juices gush forth, you've selected the right topic.. However, be careful. Make sure you are the focus of your essay, rather than who or what you're passionate about.

I made one of my students rewrite her essay featuring Nelson Mandela because it seemed to be designed to convey the greatness of the former world leader. Only in the student's last paragraph did she attempt to show how Mandela had inspired her. By then, it was too late.

already lost the admissions officers with an essay that didn't give them what they wanted to know. She would have bored them.

The student rewrote her essay, switching the focus from why to how Mandela had inspired her. Thus, the admissions officers could learn more about the applicant and perhaps less about Mandela, with whom I'm sure they already knew about anyway.

Another student had a similar problem. His parents had sent him to me because they were disappointed in his essay, which was about snowboarding. They wanted me to persuade him to write about his experience quitting his school's football team.

The young man was an excellent writer. His essay, which outlined the steps in performing a snowboard jump, was both descriptive and well-organized. I'm sure the essay would have received an A for a class assignment, but it was far from what an admissions officer would want to read.

The student told me he had quit football because he didn't want to return after he had broken his hand in a practice. When I asked him if he would have relinquished snowboarding if he had broken his hand on the slopes, he looked at me as though I were nuts. His answer confirmed his passion.

We found a way to incorporate the steps of a snowboard jump into the steps he was taking to fulfill his educational and career goals. I don't want to give away too much of his essay, but he sent me an email letting me know his acceptance rate was 100 percent. Not bad!

By focusing on your inspiration itself, rather than on who or what is the source of the inspiration, you can show admissions officers how you think and what you value. In other words, you will give them what they want.

5.) Getting Either Too Many Opinions or Getting Biased Ones

No matter how good you think your essay is, show it to someone else. Why do you think even the best professional writers have editors? There's also a saying that lawyers who defend themselves have an idiot for a client. Do not submit your essay without having someone else review it.

Make sure the people you choose are capable of this critical task. You must value their opinions and their writing abilities. Because this is your essay and your direct appeal to schools that you are applying to, don't let anyone haphazardly change your mind about your topic or how you should approach it. Keep your mind open to their suggestions, and decide whether they are valid. If you aren't sure, reconsider the suggestions the following day. Don't be stubborn about your essay, but don't be wishy-washy about it either. It's an important reflection, and you get only one chance at making a first impression. This is it.

Having one or two people who know what they're doing is enough. If you're unsure about their qualifications, choose two or three people. Once you surpass three people, problems ensue.

There's a saying that too many cooks spoil the broth. The same holds true for college application essays. When more than three people look at a piece, the incoming suggestions not only can make one's head spin, they can override the essay's voice, which is something admissions officers seek. When too many people contribute to an essay, it risks sounding as though a committee wrote it. It must reflect you.

Part 3
The Finishing Touches

9 Working backwards

If writing were just knocking out words, anyone could do it. There are three tricks to good writing: getting started, completing what you have to say, and rewriting. Skipping the last step not only can be imprudent, it can cost an acceptance.

So now that you know the tricks, how do you apply them? Whenever students seek my help, I make sure they bring a rough draft. Some show me work they consider finished; others bring me as little as a half a page of rambling thoughts. Either way, I let them know they're merely at the first stage of their writing.

We chat for a while. I not only get them comfortable with me, but I gather a sense of their personality and other characteristics. This is important for me to know because I want to make sure it's reflected in their essays. However, we talk mostly about the content of their essays. I'm not suggesting that you must hire a writing coach. However, I strongly suggest you share your essay with someone who can give you this type of feedback.

You are accustomed to writing about topics other than yourself. When you write school papers, you're required to look things up. For an application essay, you must look within. Introspection can be difficult. It requires self-awareness, patience and brutal honesty. However, I've never met anyone who said it wasn't worth the effort. The second drafts always are greatly improved, but they're seldom finished.

Sometimes the essays are difficult to understand because the ideas in them spin around as if they were captured straight from the student's brain. The writer obviously was so busy getting thoughts down, he or she might not have grasped the importance of them. When the relevance comes out, we move on to the thirdstage. This stage differs from the final stage of completing an academic essay. You don't just polish up the grammar and organization; you capture the reader's attention and leave him or her with something to remember.

I don't think any of my clients have kept the same beginning and ending they had started with. Even if the meat of their stories have held steady, often times their beginnings and endings change dramatically. I tell my students not to worry about writing a good first paragraph until the essay is finished. Most of the students find it easier to work this way. Thus, when they're finished telling their story, they can concentrate on finding a clever way to draw the reader into it.

I remember one student, however, who didn't like the technique at all. "You're making me work backwards," he kept telling me. "No," I told him. "I'm just shaking up your process a bit. It's easier to find the good stuff that way." I continued to explain to him that the first paragraph of his application essay was similar to a headline in a newspaper of magazine. If it's not interesting, the reader won't want to spend time reading the story. I've never heard of a single news organization in which the reporter wrote the story after the headline. The headline writer always works with a completed story.

Don't think of the application essay as an essay. Just write a story, one that only you can tell. This usually comes more naturally than writing an essay. Find something enjoyable to write about. Get busy, and don't waste time with the finishing touches until the end of the process even if they will be the first things read.

10 The Olympic task of a compellingessay opener

http://www.mymcmedia.org/the-olympic-task-of-a-compelling-essay-opener/

Blog Post: Feb. 8, 2014

As much of the world watched the opening ceremonies of the Olympics, I couldn't help but wonder whether the spectacle was worth a billion dollars. That's more than most of us could contemplate, much less could spend in a lifetime, even if we had it. Was it worth it?

In truth, the answer may vary depending upon who is asked. Sports fans may not think so; fans of pageantry might. A better question might be, "Why was it opened in such a grand fashion?"

The answer is simple: to draw the audience in. The Olympic planners are saying, "Pay attention. What's in store will be magnificent."

This is what I advise students when they are working on their college application essays. They must grab their audience (the admissions officers) right from the start, opening their essays in a way to encourage the reader to stay tuned.

There's a lot invested in the Olympics. It's not just the years and long hours of practice the athletes put into their sport. It's not just the facilities erected. It's not just the expense of broadcasting the event around the world. It's not just the enormous amount of security measures taken to thwart off terrorist attack. The list is mind boggling.

When the Russians decided to spend upwards of a billion dollars to open the festivities, at least for those planning it, the expense was worth it. It was a billion-dollar promise that there would be more fantastic things in store.

I'm not suggesting anyone needs to spend big bucks on an application essay, or any on writing for that matter. However, the writer must spend much effort to capture the reader's attention. Follow up that promise with a solid body of work, and then complete it with a bang.

11 Getting help

Breaking news! Adulthood doesn't happen upon reaching 18. That's just a legal thing. Maturity, at any age, is knowing when to ask for help-and being able to accept it graciously.

If you have gotten this far through this book, you are among the top students maturity-wise, no matter what anyone tells you. You're taking your college application process seriously, as you should. Going to college is a huge milestone. You should select schools that will both challenge and nurture you. Don't haphazardly decide which colleges to apply to and eventually which to attend.

I designed this book to help students like you increase their chances of getting into their "reach" schools. However, there are plenty of other resources out there:

Families

Before writing the essay, think about possible topics. Your families can help you remember situations that might be good for illustrating your personal strengths. Parents also can help you emotionally and organizationally.

Taking time to talk to them before the writing process is a great idea. Tell them what kind of help, if any, you would like. Make sure both you and your parents are firm about boundaries.

If parental feedback is too stressful or not objective enough, one of your parents might have a friend also going through this ordeal to switch places with, allowing the family friends to provide feedback to each other's children.

Older siblings, grandparents, or aunts and uncles also may be helpful. However, never let anyone else insist on what you should be writing about. Remember, it's your story.

College Counselors in High School and College

These professionals are excellent in offering the big picture about what schools seek in students.

College Consultants and Writing Coaches

These can be tremendous stress-reducers for parents by creating structure and goals. Their experience helps bring out the student's voice and strengths. They also offer insight and fresh viewpoints, similar to those of college admissions officers.

English Teachers and Writing Professionals

These people can offer insight into ways to make essays more compelling and free from errors. English teachers often recreate a college essay experience in class by assigning one as a writing assignment.

It's good when teachers swap papers with other teachers to get fresh outlooks from someone who doesn't know the student as well. The key question, which college admissions officers want answered, is "What did you learn about the student from reading the essay?"

Low-Cost Assistance

Libraries, teen organizations, writing organizations and schools may offer free or low-cost seminars or classes. Libraries and bookstores also offer books with essay samples. A word of warning, however: Admissions officers know about these books. Let a book guide you, but don't plagiarize from it.

12 Word count

http://www.mymcmedia.org/whats-the-final-word-about-the-word-count-for-essays/

Blog Post: Oct. 22, 2013

JUST AS A PICTURE CAN RELAY MEANING, A FEW GOOD WORDS CAN HAVE A BIG IMPACT

The essays on the College Board's Common Application must be between 250 and 650 words. Anything outside that range will be rejected when electronically submitted. It's that simple. Or is it?

Students get the concept, but sometimes are still uneasy about their essay's length. I helped someone whose completed essay was just under 300 words. We were both happy with it, expect he was nervous about its length. I assured him the essay wasn't missing anything. He had told the story well, and it was concise; padding it would have diluted its impact. No admissions officer wants to read essays longer than necessary.

On the other hand, I've worked with students whose essays have lacked details or examples. Illustrating something with a little story is always much better than making a flat statement with a little or no support. Sometimes this increases the word count so much we have some serious editing to perform. I show the students how their paragraphs can be tightened rather than butchered away.

The best number of words depends on what the student needs to say. It's enough words to relay a good story, but not so many to make the reader want to speed through it. Some short essays grab the reader's attention and tell a lot with relatively few words. Other short essays don't say much and the leave reader with an empty feeling about it.

Likewise, some long essays are so entertaining the reader savors each word and feels like he or she would like to meet the student. Other long essays may be boring, prompting the reader to skim through them so he can move on to better ones.

This is my ninth blog posting for Montgomery Community Media. The word count for each of my posts has been within the Parameters for the essays on the Common App. My blog has no word-count restrictions, but I have kept them within these parameters to prove to myself the range is enough to relay most stories.

By the way, at about 400 words, this is roughly my average word count for my blog posts to date. The question, however, is: How does it rank at being helpful?

13 How do I know when I'm finished?

Hooking Up With Admissions Officers began with the million dollar question: What do they want? Now I'll end it with another million dollar question: How do I know when I'm finished?

I've put together five guidelines for determining when an essay is ready to send:

1. Make sure you have answered the question posed in the writing prompt. Although this sounds easy, it can be tricky. The real question is not merely what the prompt asks, but what it seeks. Think about why the writing prompt was posed. If you have helped the admissions officers learn something introspective and interesting about yourself, you have done well.

2. Make sure you haven't made any technical mistakes. There is no excuse for bad spelling or grammar. The essays have a limited word count, so make sure your writing is filled with what you want to convey and not just padding. Remember, your views will impress, but a collection of words will not. A well written essay is easy and enjoyable to read. Admissions officer appreciate that.

3. Make sure your essay doesn't sound as though it could have come from John or Jane Doe. The essay is not a test for regurgitating answers. It is a means for colleges to learn more about their prospective students. Make sure to convey a story that is truly yours.

4. Make sure you have opening and closing paragraphs that command attention. This is not an academic essay, so do not open with a thesis statement. Try to be memorable or mildly entertaining for the admissions officer, who must read hundreds, if not thousands, of these essays during a short time period. Don't sound crazy, but don't sound bland either. Make the admissions officers want to read your story. Finish it memorably. Don't fuss over your opening and closing paragraphs until you've completed the first draft.

5. Make sure you like it. If you are confident it reveals a side of you that your test scores and GPA can't begin to show, you are on the right track.

I hope these guidelines alleviate some of the doubt in submitting your essays, and I especially hope this book has been both informative and motivating. However, my greatest hope is for you to find confidence and to enjoy writing your application.

essays. Those who have the most fun writing them tend to produce the ones that are the most fun to read. In fact, much in life is hard work that can be enjoyable with the right attitude.

Applying to college is a challenging task, but savor it. You're at a milestone that most adults envy. You're about to step through the thresholds of adulthood and progress in ways you can't yet imagine.

When the stress hits, think about the big picture. Realize that your essay is your introduction to the admissions officers-and you control it. How great is that?

In the decades to come, dig out your essay and read it again. See who you were. Then you'll better understand how you got to be the person you have become.

Enough reading. Now write.

ACKNOWLEDGMENTS

First, I'd like to thank my friends, Jonathan Salant and Rochelle Plesset, as well as my daughter, Amy Frieder, who combed my manuscript for embarrassing mistakes. Just as I tell others, when you edit your own work, it's hard not to see what you intended to write. In addition, my friends Randi Neff and Sharan Leifer offered valuable opinions regarding my Note to the Reader. I also would like to thank Robin Schuldenfrei who transformed my mental image into a beautiful book cover. I am associated with amazing people, and each contributed dearly.

Secondly, I'd like to acknowledge that I verified and clarified much of the grammar information in this book from Plain English Handbook, by JM and AK Walsh. Editing is easier for me to do than to explain, and this book helped tremendously.

Thirdly, I'd like to attribute the graphic elements of the book. The public domain photo of the Rev. Dr. Martin Luther King Jr. came from Wikimedia Commons (www.commons.wikimedia.org/wiki/File:USMC-09611.jpg).

The Italian sign urging people to pick up after their dogs came from a photo I took on a vacation. Likewise, the Sochi photo is literally a mug shot. Look closely to see the curvature of the mug. I also took the photo on the book's cover. The goofy little worm on the fishing hook found throughout the text is my doodle and interpretation of this book's theme. My worm may lack in professionalism, but I like to think it makes up for it in spirit. If you don't agree, too bad!

And last, but not least, my utmost thanks to Don Ranly, professor emeritus of the University of Missouri School of Journalism, and perfect example of a brief acquaintance who etched a lasting impression. Without his infectious enthusiasm. for getting the

words just right-and his method of drilling the grammar into his magazine editing class-I wouldn't have retained (for more than 30 years!) half the skills I possess today.

www.ingramcontent.com/pod-product-compliance
Lightning Source LLC
Chambersburg PA
CBHW020516030426
42337CB00011B/413